CLOUDS &

Lakeland's Literary Heritage

by Bob Matthews
Assistant Director, Lake District National Park Centre, Brockhole.

Jarrold Colour Publications

Lakeland is a land of contrasts. The radio weatherman has just announced that tomorrow's early mist and drizzle will give way to sunshine but that winds will increase and the outlook is 'unsettled'. The contrasts exist not only in its weather and its moods but in its places; in its people.

Towards the eighteenth-century's end when travel in Europe became increasingly difficult, so-called 'tourists' – visitors – began to discover our own island, and the Lake District was one of the more frequented places. Among these early visitors was a scattering of writers and poets. It would seem that these travellers (was it travel or travail?) came not to admire the great natural loveliness of Cumbria but, as it were, to get a great fright! The benefits of colour photography had not yet been enforced on the population and so one was unable to bore one's friends and neighbours with holiday snaps – the early visitor employed a local artist to record valleys and hills in ink and watercolour. True images were definitely *not* required and mountains just *had* to be top heavy, but times and tastes have changed.

It is a quarter of a millennium since Daniel Defoe described this area as the 'most barren and frightful of any that I have passed through in England'. The object of this book is to help today's visitor to capture scenes of literary association from this unique blend of nature's fullness and man's relentless landscape architecture.

Thomas Gray, writing his *Journal of the Lakes* in 1769, describes an awesome scene: 'the rocks at top deep cloven perpendicular by the rains, hanging loose and nodding forwards seen just starting from their base in shivers...and [I] hastened on in silence.'

Whilst eighteenth-century visitors came on foot or at best on horseback they came nonetheless in small handfuls and as individuals. Late twentieth-century technology has bestowed the benefits of motorways and jargonised our language with expressions such as 'inter-city'. The handfuls of visitors became trickles, trickles became streams and the streams increased to torrential proportions by the twentieth century.

Dorothy Wordsworth thought it noteworthy to record in her *Journal* of the early days of the nineteenth century that a wagon had passed their door along the road to Grasmere. Ten millions plus of visitors now pass that way annually. Her brother, William Wordsworth, probably did not foresee motor transport nor the space age but while he felt it vital

Below: a nineteenth-century engraving of Lodore.

that we should be in communion with nature, he could see pressures building on his 'dear native regions'. He enjoined: '... persons of pure taste who, by their visits (often repeated) to the Lakes in the North of England, testify that they deem the district a sort of national property, in which every man has a right and interest who has an eye to perceive and a heart to enjoy.'

The prophetic utterance was manifest in flesh when the 1949 National Parks Act designated, eventually, ten areas of England and Wales, of which Wordsworth's 'dear native regions' is the largest with 880 square miles. The same legislation also brought about the Lake District National Park Visitor Centre at Brockhole near Windermere, a useful starting point for any visit to Lakeland. Displays, talks and courses there help towards understanding more of the Lake District story, and 'meet the author' sessions bring writers and readers together on many occasions.

The house at Brockhole, though only ninety years old, was built by the Gaddum family. The mistress was formerly Miss Edith Potter, full cousin to Beatrix Potter of whom we shall hear more. It is probable that very early in life one has been unknowingly exposed to Lakeland literature. Several generations have now been brought up on Peter Rabbit, Jemima Puddleduck and Mrs Tiggy-

Above: Windermere – the largest lake in England.

Below: the house and gardens, Lake District National Park Centre, Brockhole, Windermere.

winkle – delightful characters from the series of tales by Beatrix Potter.

Born in fashionable Kensington, London, on 28 July 1866, Beatrix Potter's childhood had that somewhat 'repressed' quality of upper middle class sterility. Her young days were spent ensconced in the nursery with meals brought by tray from the kitchens – a lonely life which threw her into her own imaginations. Later she revelled in the privacy of coded secret writings as a *Journal* which she diligently kept between the age of fifteen and thirty.

In 1881 the Natural History Museum was opened in South Kensington and within a short time Miss Potter became a regular visitor, developing considerable talent as a watercolour artist and a great interest in natural history, eventually becoming an expert on fungi.

As was the fashionable wont of the times, the Potter family removed from city to countryside for long summer months. This was when Beatrix Potter first came to know and love the Lake District, and regular forays into fields and woodlands gave practical insight into her museum studies.

In September 1893 she wrote a letter to Noel Moore, eldest son of a former governess. He had fallen ill and, having nothing better to write about, Beatrix Potter 'the blue-eyed lady who came in a carriage with a coachman' invented a story about '. . . four little

Below: Hilltop Farm, near Sawrey, Hawkshead. Beatrix Potter's first property in the Lake District.

rabbits who lived with their mother in a sandbank...'. Thus was born Peter Rabbit, the first of the series of tales, combining her skills as a natural historian and an impressive watercolour artist.

With the publication of several books, enough money had accrued to give Beatrix financial independence of her parents. She bought Hill Top Farm, Sawrey, in the Lake District, in 1905. She was still a dutiful daughter, however, and her parents refused their permission for her marriage to Norman Warne of the publishing family (she was now aged thirty-nine!). Sadly, although they were secretly engaged, Norman died of leukaemia a few weeks later. This was a desperate blow to Beatrix, she lost herself in work, both in writing and in her new-found property in the Lake Country.

She married William Heelis of Ambleside in 1913. He was her solicitor who guided her through the acquisitions of property and land as well as being a kind and warm-hearted companion. Her 'lyric years' virtually over, they moved into Castle Cottage and she devoted her remaining decades to becoming a sheep farmer! Helen Beatrix Potter, now Mrs Heelis of Sawrey, had achieved much, bringing pleasure to countless millions. She died peacefully on 22 December 1943, her ashes being scattered at a secret location, known only to her former shepherd and his descendants.

Below: Castle Cottage where Beatrix Potter (Mrs Heelis) died in 1943. Both this and Hilltop Farm now belong to the National Trust.

As we move along from Brockhole towards Ambleside, we see a house set high above the road just beyond the Low Wood Hotel. It was to this home, Dove Nest, that Felicia Dorothy Hemans came in 1830. She was a well-known poetess of the day and, sustained by her personal faith, wrote many formerly popular hymns of praise. Now she is best remembered for lines almost equally as famous as Wordsworth's 'Daffodils': *'The boy stood on the burning deck, whence all but he had fled . . .'*. They were penned as she sat in a garden arbour looking out over some of the finest countryside to be seen anywhere.

Much of the land along here belonged to Briery Close which, in the mid nineteenth century, was the Lakeland home of Lancashire magnate Sir James Kay-Shuttleworth. It was here in August 1850 that Charlotte Brontë first met the novelist Elizabeth Gaskell. They became great friends and Mrs Gaskell became Charlotte Brontë's biographer.

The mention of Lake District and literature brings most visitors in word association to 'Wordsworth' and the 'Lake Poets'. William Wordsworth was born on 7 April 1770 in Cockermouth and is regarded as one of the most famous of Cumbria's sons. His father was agent to the Lowther Estate, the young William being educated at Hawkshead Grammar School and at Trinity College, Cambridge. The year 1788 and his first vacation saw Wordsworth returning to the Lake

Below: Dove Nest, home of Felicia Dorothy Hemans

District. His autobiographical poem *The Prelude* records something of the delight in coming back to his old stamping ground, meeting old friends and viewing familiar scenes.

The following summers found him travelling to Wales and further afield over to Switzerland and Revolutionary France. In 1791 Wordsworth again visited France and the new rampant republican politics had a significant effect on him. It was during this lengthy visit that he met Annette Vallon at Orleans. Their romance brought hostility from the Vallon family and this, together with France's declaration of war, made Wordsworth return to England before his daughter, Caroline, was born in France in December 1792.

William's sister Dorothy now began to devote herself to looking after him, both in daily practicalities and in copying out and editing his literary output. Spending some months in their native Cumberland the Wordsworths removed to the West Country in 1795, there to strike up long lasting friendships with Samuel Taylor Coleridge and Robert Southey.

In autumn 1799, Wordsworth introduced Coleridge to the delights of his native county by taking him on a walking tour beginning at Temple Sowerby in the east and, traversing mountain passes and threading through lovely valleys, they circumnavigated the

Below: Hawkshead Grammar School. William Wordsworth was at school here and, although encouraged to write, he was not encouraged to carve his signature on his desk!

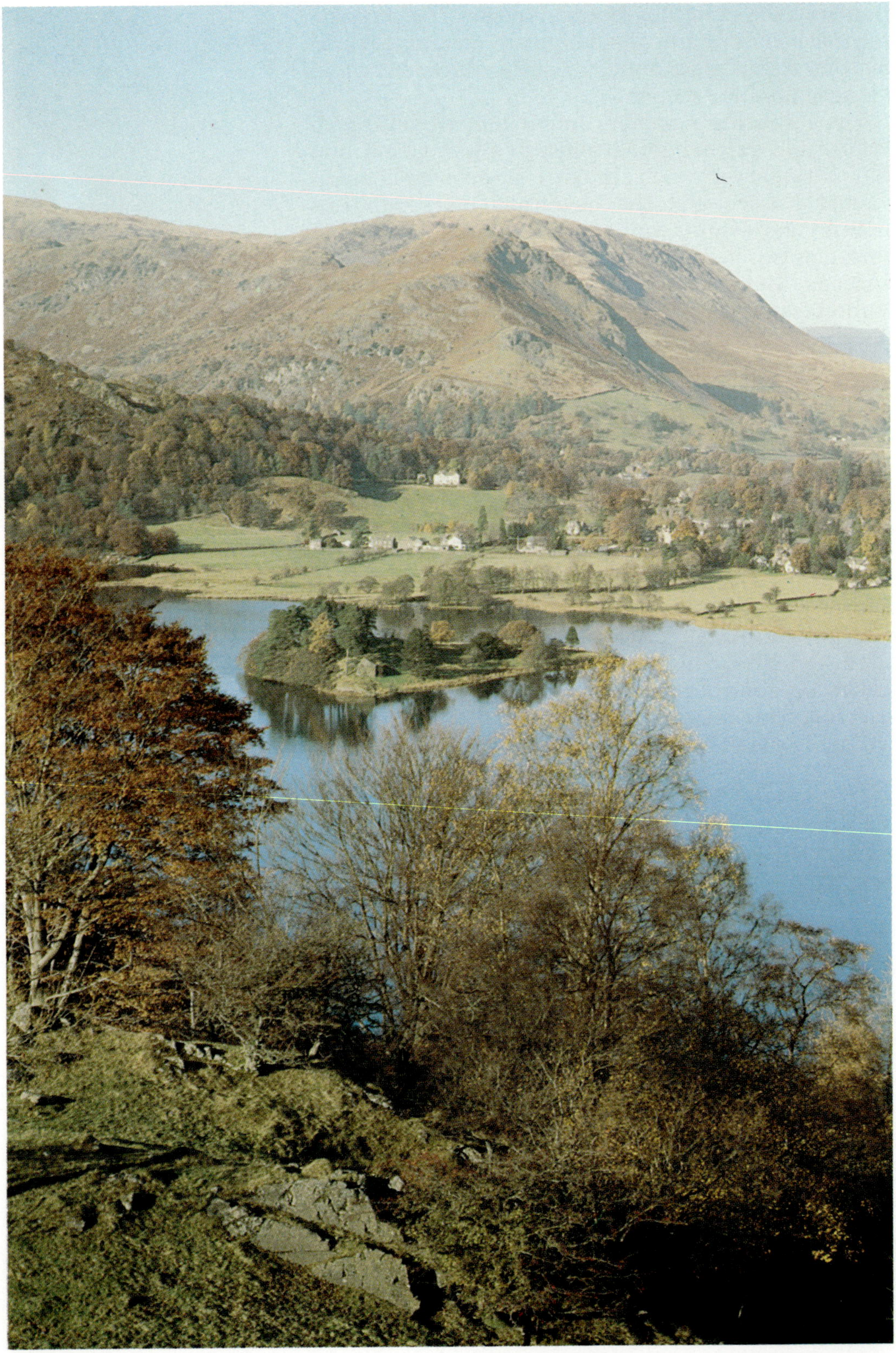

Lake Country. On the way they came upon a cottage at Townend, Grasmere to which William took an immediate liking. William wrote to Dorothy: *'Coleridge was much struck with Grasmere and its neighbourhood ... there is a small home at Grasmere empty, which, perhaps, we may take....'* They did take it and moved in during December 1799, spending over eight particularly happy years there. The cottage was formerly the Dove and Olive Branch Inn – we now know it as 'Dove Cottage'. This period may be described as Wordsworth's 'lyric years' when much of his greatest work was accomplished.

Sister Dorothy managed the Wordsworth affairs and kept an excellent record in her *Journal*, and it would seem that she had a profound effect on her brother's work. William pays tribute to Dorothy:

> *She gave me eyes, she gave me ears,*
> *And humble cares and delicate fears,*
> *A heart, the fountain of sweet tears;*
> *And love, and thought and joy.*
>
> 'The Sparrow's Nest'

Like her brother, Dorothy had a great fondness for walking. Her *Journal* is full of descriptions of these walks. She held strong views on nature and encouraged William to see that the natural world was an important influence on man. They believed that every living object lived in its own right and was to be treated with respect.

Opposite: Grasmere from Loughrigg. Wordsworth's affection for this lake is apparent from many of his poems.

Below: Dove Cottage was Wordsworth's home for his 'lyric years', but later, headquarters for twenty years of Thomas De Quincey who published *Confessions of an Opium Eater*. Here it was De Quincey had his library of 5,000 books. *'For it happens that books are the only articles of property in which I am richer than my neighbours.'*

Above: Wordsworth's Cottage at Rydal Mount, where the poet spent the last years of his life.

Below: the famous Swan Hotel, Grasmere.

William married one Mary Hutchinson on Monday 4 October 1802 at the parish church of Brompton, a village to the south-west of Scarborough in Yorkshire.

Dorothy was not at all pleased by the marriage – it meant sharing her brother with another woman! The wedding day was an anguish for her but she adapted to it and took it all in her stride, even when they were joined by Sara Hutchinson, Wordsworth's sister-in-law. However, Dorothy's literary output seems to have been stymied and she ceased to record her *Journal* within a few weeks. Three children were born to Mary and William at Townend: John, Dorothy (named after her aunt but always referred to as Dora), and Thomas.

Many other highlights manifested in visits from a whole circle of friends – Samuel Taylor Coleridge; Robert Southey; the sensitive and shy but brilliant Thomas De Quincey; Charles and Mary Lamb; and Walter Scott who, apparently very dissatisfied with the food at the Wordsworths, was wont to climb out of his bedroom window in the early morning, eat a hearty breakfast at the Swan and creep back to join the meagre repast at Dove Cottage!

The Wordsworth family had outgrown their accommodation and removed to Allan Bank in May 1808. This larger home stands above Grasmere village and while here, two more Wordsworth offspring made their appearance, a second daughter, Catherine on

6 September 1808, and on 12 May 1810, William junior was born.

The Allan Bank occupation lasted just three years and in 1811 the family moved back down the hill to The Parsonage opposite the church.

Their two-year sojourn here was marked by sad events for the Wordsworths: De Quincey's increasing opium habits, Coleridge's mutability, Sara Hutchinson, Coleridge's scrivener, was suffering severely from consumption and, worst of all, the death of two children – Catherine on 4 June 1812 and Thomas on 1 December. These events unsettled the family and they removed to Rydal Mount in 1813. Here, William Wordsworth spent the remaining decades of his life. Now rather comfortably off, he had metamorphosed from a radical free thinker (he joined the Girondists of the French Revolution), to an Establishment High Tory occupying a salaried position as Distributor of Stamps for Westmorland – 'a government sinecure'.

Whatever his politics, William Wordsworth was now well established and highly regarded and Rydal Mount became an object of pilgrimage for many hundreds of excursionists eager to catch a glimpse of the great man. The nation officially crowned his career in 1843 when he succeeded Southey as Poet Laureate. But the year 1847 saw the death of his dearly loved daughter Dora, deep sadness overcoming Wordsworth. His own death occurred on 23 April 1850 at eighty years of age. He is buried, along

Above: Wordsworth's tombstone in Grasmere churchyard.

Below: Grasmere church.

with many members of his family, in Grasmere churchyard.

Still in Rydal, Nab Cottage (left) was the home of Thomas de Quincy. Hartley Coleridge, brilliant son of brilliant father, later took over the tenancy. Deprived of his fellowship at Oriel College, Oxford, he became a London journalist, ran a school in Ambleside for a few years until it failed and settled finally at Rydal. In that time when the literary set were generally ill regarded by locals, it seems that Hartley, in spite of his persistent drunkenness, was well liked by his neighbours.

Above: this charming building in a most beautiful setting is Nab Cottage. Thomas De Quincey came a-courting Margaret Simpson here. She bore him a son and they were married in 1817.

> *He lived among untrodden ways to*
> *Rydal Lake that lead:*
> *A bard whom there were none to praise*
> *and very few to read.*

The lovely Rothay Valley has many literary associations for the enquiring visitor. This area contrasts vividly with the rather flat terrain around Rugby. Its literary associations? Dr Thomas Arnold built a holiday home here, Fox How, in 1834. He, the famed headmaster of Rugby School, was father of the poet Matthew Arnold. The book *Tom Brown's Schooldays* by Tom Hughes was dedicated to 'Mrs Arnold of Fox How'. Dr Arnold died in 1842 and is buried at Rugby School but Mrs Arnold continued to live at Fox How until her death in 1873. She is buried in Ambleside churchyard.

Below: Fox How in the lovely Rothay Valley, holiday home of Matthew Arnold. Charlotte Brontë wrote: '*The house looked like a nest, half buried in flowers.*'

The Wordsworths were prodigious walkers. They roamed the Lakeland fells and dales, finding inspiration for poetry and composition. As well as receiving many visitors to their homes in Grasmere, they themselves returned visits to their many friends, particularly to Robert Southey and the Coleridge family at Keswick. En route, they might just happen to take in the summit of Helvellyn for the afternoon!

Helvellyn – a magical mysterious name for one of England's highest mountains – a summit to which many visitors seek to achieve to take them to over 3,000 feet. One of England's airiest situations is here aspired to by fellwalkers – Striding Edge, technically an arête – a ridge flanked by precipitous cliffs.

It was from these crags that one Charles Gough of Manchester pitched headlong to a lonely, sudden death. At that time these mountains were ill frequented and his mortal remains were not discovered for some months. However, his dog faithfully stood guard over her master's bleached skeleton and the account is embodied both by Wordsworth in 'Fidelity' and by Sir Walter Scott in 'The Faithful Dog' (below).

> *I climbed the dark brow of the mighty Helvellyn...*
> *...When I marked the sad spot where the wanderer had died.*

The western sides of the Helvellyn range have their

Above: Stepping stones across the River Rothay.

Below: Striding Edge, Helvellyn.

Above: Thirlspot and the Vale of St John.

roots in Thirlmere and the Vale of St John. In Wordsworth's time Thirlmere was much different in appearance – known as Leathes Water, it was almost two small lakes whose level was raised in 1894 to bring fresh water to thirsty Manchester. St John's Vale boasts connections with King Arthur who rode over from 'Merrie Carlisle' and was beguiled by the beautiful witch Gwendoline. Entering the enchanted castle of St John he leaves England undefended until he finally breaks free of the spell. Sir Walter Scott again takes Lakeland lore and encapsulates it in his writings *The Bridal of Triermain*:

> *Know, too, that when a pilgrim strays . . .*
> *. . . Of the valley of St John.*

The eastern flanks of Helvellyn are rooted in the Ullswater valley. It was here in 1802 that the Wordsworths came to visit their friends the Clarksons. From Dorothy's *Journal*, we get an interesting background as to how a Wordsworthian composition came about:

> *Thursday April 15 1802*
> *. . . When we were in the woods beyond Gowbarrow Park, we saw a few daffodils close to the waterside . . . as we went along we saw that there were more and yet more. I never saw daffodils so beautiful.*

Below: Wordsworth's daffodils.

How many readers have struggled to learn '*I wandered lonely as a cloud . . .*' at some time in their school career? However, at this particular location now, there are sadly very few daffodils to be seen.

Having travelled the road northwards from Grasmere and Rydal through St John's we arrive at Keswick. This area is equally well steeped in literary associations. We make for Greta Hall, a building in the grounds of Keswick School and used by them. It was formerly the house of both Samuel Taylor Coleridge and Robert Southey. Mr and Mrs Coleridge and their four-year-old son, Hartley, moved there in July 1800 as their house was being completed and they paid a rent of twenty-five guineas a year. Two more children, Derwent and Sara, were born here before their father went off on his wanderings in 1804. He was the unfortunate victim of drug abuse, being addicted to opium. Perhaps his make-up portended this – a brilliant mind yoked to an irresolute and dependent character always needing the support of a constant friend.

Born on 21 October 1772, son of a Devon clergyman, Coleridge was educated (along with Charles Lamb) at Christ's Hospital School, London and later at Cambridge. The omens were bad even here, as, to get away from involvement in minor scrapes, he enlisted as a dragoon. He frittered away valuable time, writing for newspapers, preaching as a Unitarian, not settling to anything great which really was his potential, for he had a great mind. The Wedgwood family granted him an income of £150 per year but then he met the Wordsworths – William and Dorothy – in the West Country. Here at last was stimulation for Coleridge brilliance and it would seem that Dorothy acted as a catalyst for both men. They lived three miles apart – Alfoxden and Nether Stowey, Somerset – and were constantly in each other's company, a triune body almost, for Coleridge wrote, *'three people, but only one soul'*.

They agreed to write a volume of poetical works, *Lyrical Ballads*. It was published in 1798 and, while Wordsworth was to tell simple, everyday stories, Coleridge was to deal with the supernatural in common life. Thus was born what may be regarded as the Coleridge triumph – *The Rime of the Ancient Mariner*. Published by a Bristol bookseller, Cottle, the copyright was later sold with all the others on Cottle's list, to Longmans, who immediately gave it back to Wordsworth as of zero rating for value. Nevertheless, time has erected this volume as a milestone in our literary heritage.

Coleridge had become acquainted with the young Oxford student, Robert Southey, and they married two sisters, Edith and Sara Fricker. Southey was the

Above: the waterfall at Lodore, just above the head of Derwentwater. In 'Rhymes for the Nursery' (extract below), Southey describes for his children how the water comes down the cataract of Lodore:

*From its sources which well
In the Tarn on the fell;
From its fountains
In the mountains,
Its rills and its gills;
Through moss and through brake,
It runs and it creeps
For a while, till it sleeps
In its own little Lake.
And thence at departing,
Awakening and starting,
It runs through the reeds
And away it proceeds,
Through meadow and glade,
In sun and in shade,
And through the wood-shelter,
Among crags in its flurry,
Helter-skelter,
Hurry-scurry.
Here it comes sparkling,
And there it comes darkling,
Now smoking and frothing
It tumult and wrath in,
Till in this rapid race
On which it is bent,
It reaches the place
Of its steep descent.*

antithesis to Coleridge – settled, self-controlled, dutiful and industrious. He was one of the writers who made a comfortable living from his chosen career. His regular income supported not only his own family, but Coleridge's deserted fledglings and another sister in law, widowed Mrs Lovell. His respectable journalism was an adjunct to extensive children's writings and *The Three Bears* was a Southey creation.

Southey was born on 12 August 1774, moved to Greta Hall, Keswick in 1803 and was made Poet Laureate in 1813. He died on 21 March 1843, leaving a library of 14,000 books. He is buried in Crosthwaite Church at Keswick. His fellow poet Coleridge died at Highgate in London in 1834.

'In the following extract, Southey delightfully describes the view on this page:

> Pensive, though not in thought, I stood at the
>   window, beholding
> Mountain and lake and vale; the valley disrobed
>   of its verdure;
> Derwent retaining yet from eve a glassy reflection.

Above: Keswick.

Opposite: Crosthwaite Church, Keswick.

Below: Wordsworth Room, Old Windebrowe, Keswick.

A former vicar of Crosthwaite Church, Canon H. D. Rawnsley, was a progenitor of the National Trust as well as a social reformer and prolific writer. It was Rawnsley who was responsible for moving the 'Rock of Names' before it was inundated by Thirlmere's rising water. William and Dorothy Wordsworth and Samuel Taylor Coleridge had carefully carved their initials in the rock. Keswick still holds an annual 'Old Folks' Dinner' for which Rawnsley composed many sonnets.

Charles Lamb came to visit Coleridge at Greta Hall in 1802. They arrived *'in the midst of gorgeous sunshine, which transmuted all the mountains into colours . . . . We thought we had got into Fairy Land. . . . Such an impression I never received from objects of sight before. . . . Glorious creatures, fine old fellows, Skiddaw etc, I never shall forget ye. . . .'* Charles and Mary Lamb climbed Skiddaw and explored Lakeland.

Old Windebrowe, Keswick was formerly the home of Raisley Calvert, a friend to Wordsworth. Raisley fell ill and William nursed him in 1794. Sadly, the illness was fatal. Raisley bequeathed £900 to William which gave him some financial independence, thus enabling the Wordsworth career to take its selected course. The Wordsworth Rooms have been carefully restored by the Calvert Trust and are open to visitors.

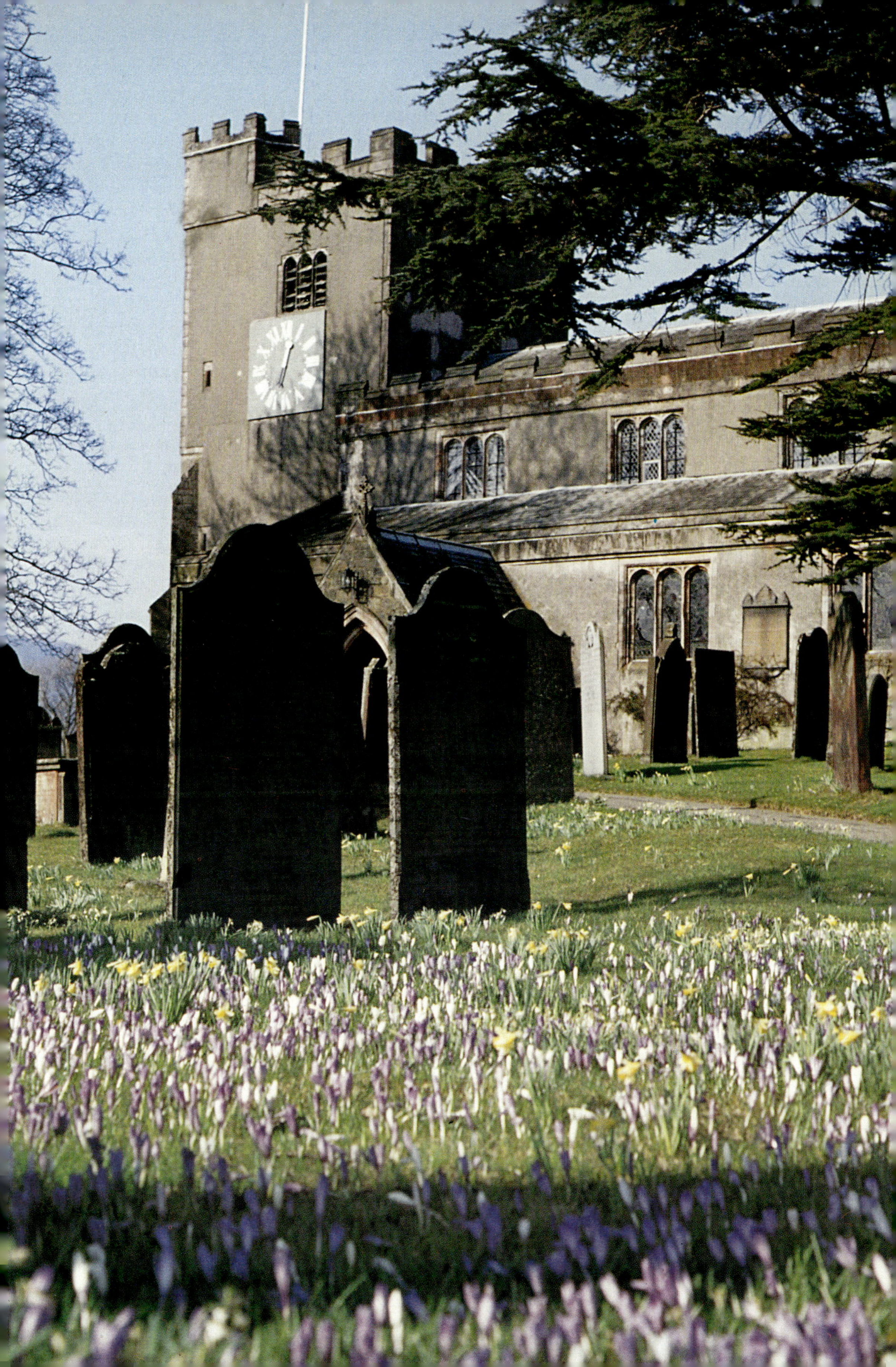

Above: Castlerigg Stone Circle.

Below: sunset over Coniston Old Man.

Castlerigg Stone Circle is a testimony to prehistoric man's existence in Cumbria. In such a fine setting, elevated above Keswick with a magnificent panorama of hills, it is a place to ruminate, as have so many writers. John Keats visited in 1818, later describing the stone circle '... *like a dismal cirque of Druid stones, upon a forlorn moor*'.

Because of the influence of the Lake Poets, many other literary figures were drawn here – Percy Bysshe Shelley came to Keswick in 1811 and lived here for three months with his sixteen-year-old bride, Harriet Westbrook. William Hazlitt, the nineteenth-century essayist, visited Keswick in 1803 for what must be described not as a flying visit but a flying departure – with local townspeople in hot pursuit! He had become over-involved with a local lady! Charles Dickens and Wilkie Collins arrived in Cumbria in 1857.

Still in the Keswick area, we move on in time from the Lake Poets to the early twentieth century when Sir Hugh Walpole came to live at Brackenburn, his 'little paradise on Cat Bells'. Born a New Zealander on 13 March 1884 of émigré English parents, Hugh Walpole was educated in England from nine years old. He remained in England and, from 1909 until his death in 1941, he wrote forty-two novels.

Rupert Hart-Davies in his biography of Walpole tells us that Sir Hugh (knighted in 1937) first came to the Lake District in 1923. One of his few regrets in life was that he hadn't been born a Cumbrian. In December 1927 he set about writing the *Herries' Chronicle*, a fictitious family imagined to be rooted in Cumberland (as it then was) in a series of novels beginning with *Rogue Herries* which appeared in 1930. The story opens in the 1720s with the Old Rogue and his son David, and their heirs and descendants are the central theme through subsequent sequels. *Judith Paris* followed in 1931; *The Fortress* in 1932; *Vanessa* in 1933. In a prefatory letter, Walpole tells us that: '*My intention is simply to record scenes from the life of an English family during two hundred years of English change and fortune and, beyond that, to pay a tribute to a part of England that I dearly love...the four books are seen together in my mind as a piece of gaily tinted tapestry worked in English colours.*'

The books record historical fact with great accuracy and the minutiae of the daily life of shepherds and snobs alike. He paints word pictures of sight, sounds and even smells of humanity – Walpole was a fastidious little bachelor.

He bought Brackenburn in 1923 – not open to the public, it is found alongside the road under Cat Bells as the road from Grange to Portinscale emerges from the woods, opening to magnificent views across Derwentwater and 'Herries Country'.

Above: Derwentwater and Keswick against a backdrop of Blencathra.

Below: Watendlath – where the redoubtable Judith Paris lived and loved in Walpole's *Herries Chronicle*.

Above: line drawing of Graham Sutton.

Sir Hugh Walpole died on 1 June 1941 at the age of fifty-seven and is buried in St John's churchyard in Keswick. Sir Hugh appreciated the compactness and variety of Lakeland and was moved to write an end paper to *Vanessa*: '*So small is the extent of this country that the sweep of the eagle's wing caresses all of it, but there is no ground in the world more mysterious, no land at once so bare in its nakedness and so rich in its luxury . . . its strong people have their feet in the soil and are independent of all men.*'

A Cumbrian writer nearer our own time is Graham Sutton (left), who eventually settled in a house under Skiddaw. He made his name by broadcasting regularly 'on the wireless' both as compère in North Regional programmes and as an actor.

He produced five historical novels, a chronicle of the Fleming family. The Flemings have two main bases: Seathwaite and Borrowdale, preceded by the family home being at Yottenfews and 'Sea Cow Field' – where? Does 'Sellafield' help you to locate it?

In chronological order the book titles are: *The Rowan Tree* – Elizabethan intrigue in Cumberland; *Shepherd's Warning*; *Smoke Across the Fell* – Iron masters of Cumberland's Industrial Revolution; *North Star* and *Fleming of Honister*. In the last book, Quarrymaster Fleming is involved with engineering the main railway line from Carlisle south over the mountains.

Below: Bassenthwaite Lake and Skiddaw.

Graham Sutton was born of a Cumberland family which had lived here for at least four centuries. He was educated at St Bees School and Queen's College, Oxford. His Fleming tale is impregnated with the smell of Cumberland earth, the rugged beauty of its fells and dales and fiercely independent and stout-hearted Cumbrians – well worth reading.

Honister Pass joins Borrowdale to Buttermere. Honister Quarries were the setting for O. S. McDonnell's 'Moses Rigg' – a quarry owner who sheltered a fugitive of injustice in his book *George Ashbury*. It is a tale of those involved in that traditional Cumbrian pastime of smuggling along remote mountain tracks and concealed byways.

Buttermere was given the title 'Secret Valley' by Nicholas Size, former mine-host at the Bridge Inn, Buttermere. Size researched the Scandinavian Settlement period in Cumbria and, at the encouragement of Hugh Walpole, embroidered his findings and wrote *Shelagh of Eskdale* and *The Secret Valley*. Published in 1932 by Frederick Warne, the books were republished in 1976 by Michael Moon of Whitehaven. They tell of the days when Norse paganism was giving way to Christianity, leading on to the suggestion that the Normans from their bases at Carlisle and Cockermouth were unable to subdue the inhabitants of Buttermere Valley and it remains the only part of England never to have been conquered.

Top: St Bees.

Above: the Gosforth Cross: the finest wheelhead cross to be found, symbolising the transition from Norse mythology to Christianity and featuring in the Nicholas Size books.

Below: Buttermere and Crummock Water.

Buttermere, Crummock Water and Loweswater drain through the lovely Vale of Lorton. John Wesley came to West Cumbria in 1759 exasperated by a 'generation of liars' en route over the 'sands' route into the south-west of the county from Lancaster. A few days later his journal records, however, *'Tues. 15th May. I rode over to Lorton, a little village at the foot of a high mountain. Many came from a considerable distance and I believe did not repent of their labour; for they found God to be a God both of the hills and valleys, and no where more present than in the mountains of Cumberland.'*

In Cockermouth can be found Wordsworth's birthplace. Born here on 7 April 1770, his father was estate agent to the Lowther family who owned vast acreages of the county and had many industrial interests as well as a castle in West Cumbria.

For those who are interested in Lakeland's literary heritage, a visit to Mirehouse out along the Bassenthwaite road is a must. For generations this typical English manor house had belonged to the Spedding family.

James Spedding (1808–81) was a man of letters, having been educated at Bury St Edmunds along with brothers Tom and Edward. Here they met Edward Fitzgerald, but James Spedding also went on to Trinity College, Cambridge where, as a member of the Cambridge 'Apostles' he met Thackeray and Arthur Hallam and struck up a lifelong friendship with

Below: Wordsworth's birthplace, Cockermouth.

Alfred Tennyson. James Spedding forsook a promising career in the Colonial Service to devote his life to a study of Francis Bacon – his research was published in fourteen volumes! Hospitality at Mirehouse was regularly extended to literary notables – Tennyson seemingly needed the Speddings' ministrations so badly that in 1835 he sold his much-prized Chancellor's Medal for English Verse for £15 so that he could get to Mirehouse. Needless to say he was impecunious at the time! Tennyson was greatly impressed by the scenery of the Mirehouse environs, and in the great work *Morte d'Arthur* Bassenthwaite influence can be detected:

> *The bold Sir Bedivere uplifted him,*
> *And bore him to the chapel in the fields*
> *A broken chancel with a broken cross,*
> *That stood on a dark straight of barren land. . . .*

(The little lakeshore church makes a delightful objective across the fields for the walker.) The Spedding brothers were befriended by Thomas Carlyle who regularly visited Mirehouse on his way home to Ecclefechan in Dumfriesshire. Carlyle undertook detailed research for his literary output. He became particularly involved with his studies on Cromwell and confided to his *'kind friend who lives sheltered about the rock of Skiddaw'* on some of his struggles. *'I pray daily for a new Oliver'* – it was his longing that the nineteenth century would produce a Cromwell.

Above: Pen Portrait of Alfred Tennyson by James Spedding.

Below: Mirehouse, home of the Spedding family.

Above: Thomas Carlyle.

Below: Carlisle Cathedral, where Sir Walter Scott was married in 1797. The truncated nave had served as a parish church since the Reformation.

By contrast several years researching Frederick the Great prompted Carlyle to write in 1857: '*If I live to get out of this Prussian scrape it is among my dreams to come to Mirehouse*'.

At Mirehouse the visitor is most welcome to wander freely through an atmosphere of pleasant hospitality and view manuscripts and letters of note.

James Spedding's father, John (1770–1851) was a school companion of Wordsworth at Hawkshead Grammar School. In 1835, James took Tennyson to meet Wordsworth at Rydal Mount. Robert Southey, Wordsworth's predecessor as Poet Laureate, was a neighbour of the Speddings and among the letters at Mirehouse is one from Southey, expressing concern at vandalism in Keswick – poets don't always have their heads in the clouds!

Carlisle is Cumbria's only city, boasting an ancient heritage of Roman occupation on a par with York and Chester although, perhaps to those who 'bend the knee to Jove' they looked on Lugavallum (Roman Carlisle) as the very frontier of their empire – Hadrian's great wall spans Albion hereabouts. Literary survival of this period is confined to Latin inscriptions on tombstones and fallen masonry. While the Danes burnt Carlisle in 874 and the Normans built a castle which is still in use almost a millennium on, Carlisle has featured more in military conflict than possibly any other British city.

Sir Walter Scott was a frequent visitor to Carlisle – *en passant* – and in Cumberland he met his future wife, an attractive French refugee Charlotte Charpentier whom he married in 1797 in the Cathedral.

'Back o' Skiddaw' land, to the north of Keswick, is hunted by the Blencathra foxhounds and was made famous by an almost legendary character and Cumbria's most famous song, 'D'ye ken John Peel with his coat so grey?' (Note 'grey' – not hunting pink – his coat was made of undyed Herdwick wool.) Hunting, to hard-drinking and uncouth John Peel was a compulsion and bore no relation to the rituals of the shire-county socialising and riding to hounds. John Woodcock Graves wrote the song in admiration of his older friend. John Peel is buried in Caldbeck churchyard but John Woodcock Graves impetuously emigrated to Tasmania.

Moving down the west coast the traveller arrives at Millom and we meet Norman Nicholson, present day-poet and writer of note. Having always lived in his home town, he has seen industrial depression, growth, recession and final decay during his own lifetime. He ably comments on his own observations of Millom's wax and wane in his verse.

He has commented that sickness made him a poet. Born in 1914, he fell victim in early life to a respiratory illness which enforced inactivity and limited his horizon to Black Combe, the great mountain backdrop to Millom. Had he not experienced this he assumes that he would have been a miner or ironworker as was the norm in Millom.

However, physical weaknesses constrained him to think, to look and see, to hear and listen. Thus, he began to write verse, and the first of many books, *Five Rivers*, was published in 1944 and was awarded the Heinemann Prize. Norman Nicholson's writing is not all versification however, he has written superb non-fiction books on Cumbria with respect to all aspects of the area's story. Well-researched sections on geology, glaciation, natural history and socio-economic histories have enlightened many a visitor reading *Greater Lakeland, Portrait of the Lake District* or *The Lakers*. His keen awareness of the interaction of natural processes in shaping the land and its people underlies his prose as well as his poetry. For those who have heard Norman speak, his unforgettable readings in his distinctive voice may have included the sentences: 'At bottom the Lake District is a piece of rock. It's the rock which made the land and the land that's made the people.' Perhaps in much of his work we detect that Norman is comparing the almost insignificant rate of change in nature with the cataclysmic and helter-skelter pace of life as we know it. One of the most popular Lake District books of recent years is an anthology compiled by Norman Nicholson.

> *He knew beneath mutation of year and season,*
> *Flood and drought, frost and fire and thunder,*
> *The blossom on the Rowan and the reddening of*
>   *the berries,*
> *There stands the base and root of the living rock –*
> *Thirty thousand feet of solid Cumberland.*
>   Norman Nicholson, 'To the Duddon'

Duddon Valley was also the source of inspiration for 'The Duddon Sonnets' by Wordsworth and, much more recently, the scenario for the *Plague Dogs* by Richard Adams, published in 1977.

Mention Arthur Ransome and for most the thought *Swallows and Amazons* springs immediately to mind. How many children haven't imagined themselves into the parts of Titty or Roger? – gliding into

Above: Rowan berries. The Rowan, or Mountain Ash, has featured in much of Lakeland's literature. It has a very handsome form and is frequently seen as a solitary specimen. The name 'Rowan' is related to the word 'Rune' since the tree was once credited with magical powers against witches.

unknown waters; castaways on desert islands; dealing with pirates and cut-throats; young adventure which for most is stifled by convention when growing up. For some of us, young adventure doesn't end, we are honest enough to admit to it but control it, escaping into it whenever possible!

Arthur Ransome was born on 18 January 1884, his father being a Professor of History at what became the University of Leeds. Arthur was sent to a Lake District prep school where he was bullied unmercifully. His delight was the family holidays spent at Nibthwaite near Coniston – nothing else equalled the pleasure of these weeks. After being made to sit to their first meal at their holiday home Arthur was then 'free in paradise'.

His literary career began in 1904 as a freelance literary hack, but to think of his experience being circumscribed by small-time book reviews and odd column inches would be a mistake. After impoverished years mixing with G. K. Chesterton and Hilaire Belloc, Arthur Ransome wrote a biographical account of Oscar Wilde in 1912 for publisher Martin Secker. A difficult libel suit was brought against

Below: Wastwater: England's deepest lake holds the roots of its highest mountain and has featured in many works of fiction. Wasdale also features in non-fiction and technical works as it exhibits classic landscape features.

Ransome but he won and went on to travel in Russia where he learnt the language and recorded much of its folklore.

He married his first wife, Ivy, in 1900 and a daughter, Tabitha, was born a year later. However, Arthur and Ivy were ill suited, and when an opportunity arose he returned to Russia as a reporter for the *Daily News*, reporting on the Revolution. The Bolsheviks were anxious to soften up British journalists, particularly, and Ransome became closely acquainted with Trotsky and even more closely with Evgenia, Trotsky's secretary, whom he eventually married.

Arthur Ransome's views on the Russian Revolution conflicted with those of the Cadbury family who owned the *Daily News* and Ransome and the 'News' parted company. Ransome took up an invitation from the *Manchester Guardian* to be 'Special Correspondent', but by 1930, Arthur Ransome, adventuring journalist, had become Arthur Ransome, storyteller, and he and his beloved wife moved to Low Ludderburn near Windermere. The next fifteen years saw the *Swallows and Amazons* series of stories written and published – *Coot Club*; *Winter Holiday*; *Peter Duck* and so on. Arthur Ransome died in June 1967 and is buried in Rusland churchyard, a secluded spot chosen by him.

Above: Arthur Ransome's gravestone in Rusland churchyard.

Below: the River Duddon and Duddon Valley near Ulpha.

The village of Coniston owes much of its growth to the mineral wealth locked in the surrounding fells. Slate quarrying continues and signs of former vast copper workings are abundant. These led W. G. Collingwood to romanticise local history in the novels *Dutch Agnes, Her Valentine*, along with *Thorstein of the Mere* and *The Bondwomen*, now out of print but available in libraries and sometimes in antiquarian bookshops.

In Coniston churchyard lies buried a remarkable man, John Ruskin, who spent the last thirty years of his life living on Coniston Water's eastern shore at Brantwood, a name which means 'steep wood'. Born in London 18 February 1819 to a family whose fortunes were made trading in sherry, John Ruskin was brought up in a deeply religious, Christian home. The family travelled regularly and the young Ruskin was brought to the Lake District, once, to see Robert Southey the Poet Laureate, at Crosthwaite Church, Keswick. He was much impressed by Lakeland and in later life continued these visits until he settled at Brantwood in 1871 when he was fifty-two.

John Ruskin was blessed with an encyclopaedic intelligence and a tremendous clarity of perception. He observed nature with keen insight, taking interest in all branches of natural science but was particularly fond of minerals, their form and colour.

Above: Coniston Village.

Below: Brantwood, former home of John Ruskin.

Although he was first a poet, he was also a writer and art critic, a student of architecture, as well as an artist of note and had far-seeing ideas on social injustice and reform. Some of his views were expressed in a series of articles condemning exploitation of working people which produced a self-perpetuating minority of wealthy citizens. Was Ruskin way ahead of his time? – whatever the answer, it was necessary to have his books lying around in one's home if one was to evidence any refinement!

John Ruskin's works seem to have been sadly neglected in recent decades but are just beginning an upturn with the establishment of the National Ruskin Centre at Brantwood, a fitting tribute to a man who had an Oxford college named after him, whose writings led to a modern political party being formed, and who influenced the founders of the National Trust and those who wished to share the beauties and intricacies of the countryside with their fellow men. *'The highest and first law of the universe – and the other name of life is, therefore, "help". The other name of death is "separation".'*

Much of the mark of Ruskin genius was his ability to switch in midstream from detailed discourses on one topic to some entirely unrelated subject. However, colouring all of his writings is his constant resort to his moral preaching. In the early 1870s the weather worsened over several years and Ruskin analogised this temporary climatic change to the moral and blasphemous decline of society. His thoughts were delivered as *'Stormcloud of the nineteenth century'*. His journal had recorded such daily weather reports as: *'... a fearfully dark mist all afternoon, with steady, south plague-wind of the bitterest, nastiest, poisonous blight'*, and: *'Sunday August 17th 1879. Raining in foul drizzle, slow and steady; sky pitch dark; diabolic clouds over everything'*.

Sadly, John Ruskin was wearing out, his mind was breaking down and, lovingly cared for at Brantwood by his cousin Joan Severn, his last years were spent without writing or taking observations, in fact, he scarcely remembered relatives and friends. He died peacefully on 20 January 1900. His own words would have made a fitting epitaph: *'He only is advancing in life whose heart is getting softer, whose blood warmer, whose brain quicker, whose spirit is entering into living peace'*.

There are many successful writers who still live and work in the Lake District: Melvyn Bragg; Irvine

Above: Melvyn Bragg. This popular writer and broadcaster was born at Wigton in 1939. He retreats to his Cumbrian home whenever possible. Many readers of Melvyn Bragg's novels try to identify the fictitious villages with real life counterparts.

Opposite: snow-covered mountains rise above a frosted landscape at Ambleside.

Hunt; John Wyatt; Chris Bonington; Hunter Davies and Margaret Forster, to name but a few. All find inspiration in the Lakeland scenery, in its many moods, and in its people.

It has been estimated that some fifty thousand books and literary works feature the English Lake District. It is hoped that this book will encourage the interested visitor to discover further details of local authors and places of literary association. There are many such places to visit (see inside front cover) and, morbidly, there are headstones to see.

Many of the Lake District's most notable writers may lie buried in churchyards but their works live on, to be read, loved and remembered, as long as there are books and people like us to read them.

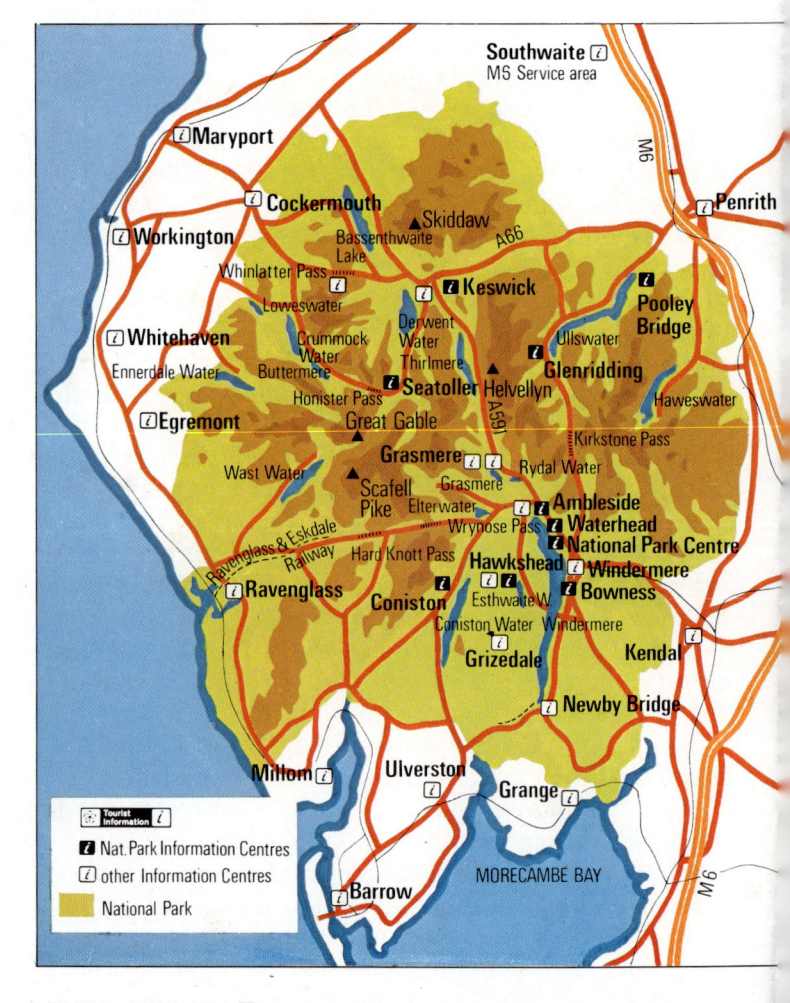

ISBN 0-7117-0189-X

© 1985 Jarrold Colour Publications.

Printed and published in Great Britain by Jarrold and Sons Ltd, Norwich. 185.